AMERICAN
WITCHES

Angie Timmons

Enslow Publishing
101 W. 23rd Street
Suite 240
New York, NY 10011
USA

enslow.com

Published in 2020 by Enslow Publishing, LLC
101 W. 23rd Street, Suite 240, New York, NY 10011

Library of Congress Cataloging-in-Publication Data

Names: Timmons, Angie, author.
Title: American witches / Angie Timmons.
Description: New York : Enslow Publishing, 2020. I Series: Creatures of the paranormal I
  Includes bibliographical references and index. I Audience: Grades 5–8.
Identifiers: LCCN 2019008573I ISBN 9781978513662 (library bound) I
  ISBN 9781978513655 (pbk.)
Subjects: LCSH: Witches—United States—Juvenile literature.
Classification: LCC BF1573 .T56 2019 I DDC 133.4/309—dc23
LC record available at https://lccn.loc.gov/2019008573

Printed in the United States of America

To Our Readers: We have done our best to make sure all websites in this book were active and appropriate when we went to press. However, the author and the publisher have no control over and assume no liability for the material available on those websites or on any websites they may link to. Any comments or suggestions can be sent by email to customerservice@enslow.com.

Portions of this book originally appeared in *Witches in America* by J. Elizabeth Mills.

CONTENTS

INTRODUCTION

Harry Potter may have introduced a new era of witchy interest to generations of readers, young and old, but the popular series based on the young wizard is hardly the first time witches and wizards have captivated an audience. Prehistoric caves have been found that show magic rituals, and throughout most of recorded history, witches have taken many forms. They can be found in folklore, literature, and other creative works.

Some notions about witchcraft can be traced to early cultures that believed in deities or spirits that controlled all aspects of their lives. Those cultures, both ancient and more contemporary, were concerned with pleasing these powerful deities. As such, they developed fears about malevolent beings, both physical and unseen, that they believed had magical powers to cause harm and displease the all-powerful deities.

History is also filled with stories of healers (people who had knowledge of the healing arts before the advent of modern medicine) and of people who were perceived as threats to the religious order and accused of witchcraft, violently persecuted, and killed.

So, how did American culture go from historical periods in which witches were hunted down and persecuted to the modern

Witches have long been the subjects of fairy tales, folklore, and entertainment. They've been portrayed in many forms, from evil villains to enchanting spell casters.

era, in which witches and wizards are beloved icons in literature and film and common Halloween costumes? Much of it comes down to knowledge.

Today, people understand how illnesses occur and how natural disasters happen. Humans have refined methods for medicine and food production based on science and evidence. Throughout much of history, however, people didn't understand things that are taken for granted today. When disaster or illness struck, people looked for someone to blame. Accused witches often found themselves on the wrong end of that blame game. And while many modern societies exercise religious tolerance, that hasn't always been the case. For instance, in Europe during the Middle Ages, hundreds of people the Christian church found threatening were accused of witchcraft and burned at the stake.

Despite these unfortunate times in history, witches have remained a fascination across many cultures and have become popular in everything from children's books to movies. There are even modern-day "witches": Wiccans, members of an earth-based pagan religion called Wicca, are sometimes called benevolent witches. Wiccans' beliefs are based on ancient polytheistic worship practices, and many of them believe in magic.

Whether modern-day "witches" or anyone else throughout history can actually make magic happen is up for debate, but interest in witchcraft has survived the test of time. Not only are people less intimidated by witches than previous generations were, interest in witchcraft and magic holds a deeper meaning for many people:

Magic holds the possibility of unlocking the world's mysteries or affecting changes in the physical world (as Wiccans believe). Others enjoy the ideas of witchcraft and magic because they like to escape into fantasies in which people can do extraordinary things—like Harry Potter.

Whatever the reason for people's interest in witchcraft, witches have an incredible history and hold a place of honor in creative expression.

1

WHAT IS A WITCH?

Wands, broomsticks, capes, pointy hats, spell books, and animals capable of helping out with magic were part of Harry Potter's world, a world in which he learned magic at a school known only to other witches and wizards. Though those aspects of his world were adapted in fun new ways for the series, they're also aspects commonly associated with witches in folklore dating back hundreds of years. In fact, when many people think of a witch, images of a cackling old woman, pointy hats, broomsticks, and wands probably come to mind, along with black cats and cauldrons of boiling potions. In the Netflix show *The Chilling Adventures of Sabrina,* however, witches are often shown dressing in modern clothes and living in regular houses where they cast spells, fight demons, and travel outside their bodies—without magic wands or pointy hats.

Both the *Harry Potter* and *Sabrina* versions of witches, as well as versions of witches in stories both old and new, captivated readers and audiences. But what's a witch, really?

BEWITCHING WORDS

The word "witch" comes from the Old English word "wicca." "Wiccian" is another Old English word meaning to cast a spell or bewitch someone. "Witch" typically refers to someone, usually a woman, who practices magic or casts spells.

Nearly every culture has legends about witches. Each portrayal is unique. Sometimes, witches are good and practice "white" (healing) magic. In other cultures, witches are believed to perform "black" magic (evil spells that harm people). Synonyms for "witch" include "sorceress," "magician," "mage," and "enchantress."

SUPERSTITIONS

A superstition is a belief about something or someone that is not based on fact, but upon rumor or popular opinion. One popular superstition is that if a black cat crosses a person's path, he or she will have bad luck. This isn't based on fact, but some people have had bad luck after seeing a black cat, and so the superstition was born.

Superstitions about witches have been around for centuries, in the United States and beyond. Many of these unfounded beliefs centered on village women who possessed certain types of medicinal knowledge before the advent of modern medicine.

FROM HEALERS TO HAGS

In the centuries before modern medicine, village women with medicinal knowledge (sometimes called "healers") could tell which plants were harmful and which would soothe a burn. They could brew a tea that would make a person calm or aid digestion, and they could dress a wound to help it heal by using crushed herbs. Other women were midwives. At a time when there were few doctors, midwives would tend to pregnant women and help them through the complicated procedure of childbirth. Much of their valuable knowledge was considered by some societies to be a form of good witchcraft, and the "witch" and her practices were generally tolerated. Unfortunately, during the eras in which village healers lived, superstition overshadowed what little scientific and medical knowledge existed. Like most of their fellow villagers, many healers were likely illiterate, relying on knowledge that was often passed down orally through generations. However, if healers' remedies didn't work, they drew the suspicion of the communities in which they lived. Accusations of dark magic started and grew quickly, resulting in trouble for the "witch." Suspicions about how healers possessed their knowledge spiraled out of control, with many believing healers were capable of hurting people with the help of evil spirits or malevolent spells recorded in spell books. Even worse, these "witches" were often believed to be earthly agents of the Devil.

PRESUMED POWERS

When superstitions and fears of the Devil reigned supreme, witches were thought to possess a wide range of powers. They were blamed

This artwork by German physician Eucharius Rosslin (1470–1526) was published in a 1513 book about childbirth. For centuries, "witches" were healers and midwives who were often the only people in their villages who knew how to handle medical needs, such as helping women during childbirth.

This eighteenth-century painting by Francisco de Goya (1746–1828), *Witches' Sabbath*, portrays the time period's belief that witches were associated with the Devil (depicted here as a goat).

for stormy weather and destroying crops (called "blasting"). They were believed to be capable of casting spells using secret words, either written or spoken. Everyone is familiar with the legend that witches can fly. Some believed witches used an ointment containing bat blood and poisonous plants that, when applied to an ordinary object, gave that object the ability to take flight. Several notable incidents of presumed witchcraft involved the witch tormenting others mentally and physically, either through the use of spells or by dispatching evil spirits. The most damning presumption was that a witch derived powers from the Devil. If a member of the community (such as a witch) had a presumed relationship with the Devil, others would be terrified that the wrath of God would be visited on their crops, their health, and all aspects of their lives. The belief that a witch's powers were derived from the Devil stirred up hysterical persecution of accused witches throughout the Middle Ages and even into the Victorian era.

THE REAL DEAL

Throughout the vast majority of humanity's long history, people knew little about science. They relied on religious or spiritual beliefs to explain the often scary, unpredictable world around them. Events they didn't understand and couldn't explain with religion were highly suspicious. Most people knew little about plants and even less about the human body. As Christianity, especially Christian sects who took the Bible very literally (such as Puritans), grew people who possessed knowledge of the medicinal value of plants

Sometimes called "witches," modern-day practitioners of Wicca, a nature-based spiritual religion, gather to meditate and connect with nature through various rituals.

and the human body became increasingly mistrusted. They were suspected of being witches who used magic to heal or harm.

Witches continue to practice today as Wiccans. Wiccan witchcraft is very different from the terrifying witches' sabbaths associated with the black-magic witches commonly depicted in popular media. Wicca is a "white" magic. Its main purpose is to heal and connect with the world through nature and the cycle of seasons.

2

TOOLS OF THE TRADE

Depending on the story, witches can tell the future, conjure potions that make people fall in love or even die, fly, and transform themselves into animals. With all these many powers, what do witches use in their magic? Customary items include a broom, a wand, and a cauldron. But how are they used, and why are witches commonly associated with black cats?

HANDY ITEMS

In the nineteenth-century German fairy tale "Hansel and Gretel," two young siblings are kidnapped by a forest-dwelling, flesh-eating witch who lures them with a house constructed of sweets. While a witch's house is most likely not made out of gingerbread and it's unlikely witches ate humans, some items are iconic and have significance in cultural ideas about witches.

Witches are usually depicted using their magic to
fly through the night sky on broomsticks.

BROOMSTICKS

Maybe the most recognizable item associated with a witch is a
broom. Brooms are obviously used for sweeping and cannot fly.
But some belief systems hold that the act of sweeping has magical significance and can summon or banish different kinds of
energy over a threshold. The idea of flying on a broomstick may
have originated with the belief in a soul's journey from the real
world to the spirit world. Some historians believe the broomstick

and witch association may originate from an old practice in which women left their brooms outside their doors to indicate they were not at home.

A MAGICAL COOKING POT

In the days before electricity and modern cooking devices, many homes had a big, black cooking pot hanging over a fire. These pots hung by a curved handle on a hook, and flames would heat the bottom and sides to cook the contents. This was a cauldron, an old-fashioned iron pot used for cooking. In witch lore, cauldrons were used for brewing potions and casting spells. In Shakespeare's play *Macbeth,* three witches recite a spell as they stand around a cauldron: "Double, double toil and trouble; fire burn and cauldron bubble." Eerie ingredients such as eye of newt and leg of toad or other unsavory items are thrown in and stirred with just the right spell to make something happen.

ITEMS OF LEGEND

In fairy tales, bad witches and evil spirits use various items to do harm. In "Sleeping Beauty," an evil fairy casts a spell in which Sleeping Beauty will prick her finger on a spinning wheel and die when she turns eighteen. In "Snow White," the beautiful Snow White is bewitched by an evil queen disguised as a hag. She convinces Snow White to eat a poisoned apple. As in these fairy tales, other items not commonly associated with everyday households are associated with witches.

A MAGIC WAND

A witch's wand is thought to direct magical energy and aid in casting spells. Traditionally made of hazel wood, wands may be made of all kinds of wood, and some witches believe the type of wood affects the outcome of the incantation. Wands may be plain or ornamented with stones and feathers. They may have carvings of letters and runes (symbols with magical significance) that aid in the practice of magic.

FAMILIARS

In popular belief, witches had animal companions, called familiars, that assisted in casting spells and other magical duties. These animal partners had close bonds with their owners, and witches were believed capable of shape-shifting into their familiars. The most common critters believed to be familiars included bats, toads, ravens, rats, and rabbits. Familiars were thought to have their own magical powers, making them even more dangerous. Popular belief

BOOK OF SHADOWS

According to many legends, a Book of Shadows, sometimes called a "grimoire," is a witch's reference. In this book a witch will write spells, experiments, and findings. Possession of any magical object was regarded with suspicion, however, and was kept hidden, hence its name. Witches kept their books in the shadows to avoid detection. It's important to remember that during the centuries when witches fell under suspicion, however, many people were illiterate and would have been unable to read a book of any kind.

was that familiars were given to witches by the Devil or by another witch and that these animals carried out orders in exchange for milk or blood.

Cats are the most iconic of all animals thought to be witches' familiars. Aloof, independent animals that don't seem to need humans in the way that dogs do, cats were easy to associate with eccentric women who kept to themselves. Whatever the reason, cats, especially black cats, represent magic or significance for many cultures, from ancient Egypt to modern day. A woman who owned several cats and kept to herself was often viewed with suspicion and avoided. She was an outcast. Unfortunately, to this

Cats, especially black cats, are the familiars most associated with witches and witchcraft.

day, black cats are victimized by centuries-old folklore about witches. Black cats often have difficulty getting adopted due to long-held, incorrect superstitions about their evil nature, and some even come to harm as part of Halloween pranks.

A TOOL FOR PROTECTION

Early America experienced several notable persecutions of accused witches. A 2009 excavation in Governor Printz State Park in Essington, Pennsylvania, showed so-called witches were not the only ones relying on objects for help. The excavation found a glass bottle with six round-headed pins inside, sealed with a wooden plug. Its construction and upside-down burial appear connected with an English "white witchcraft" charm to ward off witchcraft-related pain and was most likely put underground in the mid-eighteenth century. No others like it have been found in the United States, though other settlers from England likely used this protective measure against witchcraft.

3

TERROR IN MASSACHUSETTS BAY COLONY

In the seventeenth century, a group of strict Christians called Puritans settled in colonial New England to escape religious persecution in England. Settling mostly in the Massachusetts Bay Colony, the Puritans lived in tight-knit communities where the word of God dictated every aspect of their lives.

FROM DEVOUT TO DEADLY

Beginning in the bleak winter of 1692, the Massachusetts Bay Colony Puritans became the center of one of history's most notable persecutions. A group of young girls accused members of the colony of being witches. In the end, more than 150 people were accused, 19 people were hanged, several more died in prison, and one man was crushed to death. How did this happen?

PURITAN PRIORITIES

Understanding the witch hunts and persecutions in the Massachusetts Bay Colony begins with understanding more about the people who lived there. Puritans led severe lives. The environment in early colonial America was harsh and unforgiving. Puritans worked long hours and allowed themselves few comforts. The Puritan community rewarded conformity, a societal expectation in which all members behave the same, follow the same rules, share the same beliefs, and know their places. Clothing was simple and monochrome to avoid attention and vanity, a deadly sin. The meetinghouse was the place of worship and the center of the Puritan community. The main book in every home—and probably the only book in most homes—was the Bible, which dictated how people lived. Anyone who stood out or didn't follow the rules was not to be trusted.

PURITAN PARANOIA

Puritans feared God, but they feared the Devil just as much. They believed the Devil was real and wanted to do harm—and had the power to do so through earthly agents. This led to strongly held superstitions and a rampant and unyielding paranoia about magic, witches, and witchcraft—a practice thought to involve dealing with the Devil.

The main economy at the time was farming. Settlers depended on harvests and livestock in an unforgiving climate. If a cow fell ill or a crop failed, they believed it was God's will or those misfortunes happened because someone cursed them. Puritans were highly suspicious of one another, especially over land disputes, a frequent issue.

A FORTUNE-TELLING MISFORTUNE

Winter nights in Salem were long and cold. Children were often idle during these bleak nights. In the upstanding household of Reverend Samuel Parris, a West Indian slave named Tituba passed the evenings telling fortunes and fantastical stories to two girls, Abigail Williams and Betsy Parris. These meetings were secret because these activities were forbidden. For reasons still unknown, the girls began acting strangely. They shrieked and fell on the floor, shaking, and complained someone was pinching them. The reverend, who had a reputation for his terrifying sermons about the Devil and for fanning the flames of dislike among his fellow villagers, demanded answers. Fearful of being punished for their secret storytelling nights with Tituba, the girls accused Tituba of bewitching them. Tituba, equally afraid of retribution, immediately pleaded guilty to witchcraft and claimed other witches dwelled in the community. The wave of accusations began, with eleven other young girls joining Abigail Williams and Betsy Parris in making accusations.

THE ACCUSED AND THE TRIALS

Two female outcasts were the next to be accused: Sarah Good, a local homeless woman known for begging, and Sarah Osborne, who rarely attended church.

In the spring, a court was hastily set up to hear the accusations and decide the fates of the accused. The trials were famously dramatic. The girls would stare into space, declaring they were seeing a specter of the witch's familiar up in the rafters of the meetinghouse. They'd fall to the ground and shake, begging their "tormentor" to stop hurting them. They'd scream and utter nonsensical words. Only when the accused person was removed from the room or ordered to stay still would the "affliction" stop. The girls' reactions to the presence of the accused at court were frightening, whipping the community into a frenzy of fear and suspicion.

Old Tituba the Indian.

The Salem witch hysteria allegedly began with forbidden meetings between young girls from the colony and a fortune-telling slave from Barbados, Tituba, who was later labeled a witch.

Accusations flew, directed not just at outcasts but at well-regarded citizens, like Martha Corey, a regular churchgoer. If even their piety couldn't protect them, people wondered who was safe.

SENTENCING BEGINS

In June, Governor William Phipps assembled a Special Court of Oyer (which means "to hear") and Terminer (which means "to decide") to preside over the witchcraft cases. The first person sentenced was Bridget Bishop, an outspoken, independently minded woman who dressed strangely, had been married three times to husbands with whom she fought openly, and ran a tavern in her house—sinful behavior in the Puritan community. Bishop's tavern and lands were successful while others suffered, a sore point in Salem. Bishop pleaded innocent of witchcraft, but the girls' accusations went unquestioned. Bishop was the first person hanged on a hill that

The young girls in Salem who had accused various women of witchcraft put on quite a show during the trials, acting as though they were afflicted by the witches' evil.

Without the benefit of fair trials, many accused "witches" were executed in Salem based almost solely on the claims made by some of the colony's young girls. The Puritan minister Reverend George Burroughs, drawn here saying a prayer before his hanging, died on August 19, 1692.

would become known as Gallows Hill. The sentencing and accusations continued. By the end of September 1692, the jails were full and nineteen people had been hanged.

SPECTRAL SUSPICION

Increase Mather, a respected minister and president of Harvard College, had written extensively on witchcraft. He objected to the use of "spectral evidence," testimony about dreams and visions, in the witchcraft courts to convict the accused. Mather questioned the trustworthiness of such evidence. The governor agreed with Mather's suspicions and decreed no further witchcraft arrests were allowed. He dismantled the court in October and released the imprisoned.

WHAT CAME AFTER

All who'd been imprisoned for witchcraft were pardoned by May 1693. When the trials were over, many of the people who'd participated, including a judge, publicly stated they had been wrong

QUESTIONS REMAIN

Historians have debated how the Salem witch trials happened, and especially why the accusing girls did what they did. Could it have been illness that caused visions or mental illness? Did they make it up and, fearful of being caught lying, keep the story going? Did their parents force them to make accusations against enemies? Was it for attention in their dreary, male-dominated society? Only one girl behind the slew of accusations, Ann Putnam, apologized. She'd accused sixty-two people of witchcraft. She wrote a public apology in 1706, claiming Satan had deceived her into wrongfully accusing people of witchcraft.

and felt remorseful. On January 14, 1697, the colony held a day of fasting and reflection on the tragedy of Salem's witch trials. In 1702, a general court declared the trials had been unlawful. Nine years later, Massachusetts colony passed a bill that returned to the accused their good names and all their rights, including financial restitution to their descendants. A formal apology from the state of Massachusetts, however, did not come until 1957.

Because of the nature of their alleged crimes, the bodies of those who were hanged were not buried in consecrated ground, such as a church cemetery. What happened to their bodies is unknown, but it is believed some families claimed their loved ones and buried them elsewhere. Modern-day Salem features a memorial honoring the victims of the witch trials.

4

MORE AMERICAN WITCH HUNTS

The Salem witch trials are the best-known witchcraft-related event in American history, but Salem is far from the only persecution of so-called witches that happened in early America. Colonial America had a long and involved history of false accusations and unfounded executions that happened before the Salem witch trials and after. Interestingly, no actual witches were ever found. Only innocent people were accused, jailed, and killed.

COLONIAL CONNECTICUT

About fifty years before the Salem trials, Connecticut went through witch hysteria. Fears of the forces of evil and witchcraft, fueled by earlier European persecutions and strict religious practices, was common in early Puritanical New England. Colonists also had violent conflicts with Native Americans over land, epidemics, natural disasters, uncertainty about the government, and other difficulties. Times were hard, and people needed a scapegoat on which to focus their frustrations.

HARTFORD

The first known North American witchcraft trial and execution took place in Connecticut in 1647. Little is known about the victim, Alse Young, except she was married and had a daughter (who would be accused of witchcraft thirty years later in Massachusetts). No one knows why she was accused, though some speculate she may have been blamed for a deadly influenza epidemic that struck in early 1647.

Alse was the first victim of what would become known as the Hartford Witch Panic. Between 1648 and 1663, thirty-four people were put on trial. Nearly half of them were convicted and hanged.

In 1655, Governor John Winthrop, the son of the governor of Massachusetts and one of the most popular doctors in New England, intervened in the trials, decreeing that no more accused witches were to be executed.

A VOICE OF REASON

Winthrop had an interesting insight into witchcraft. He was familiar with forms of earth-based magic such as astrology and alchemy. He knew how difficult it was to perform any kind of real magic;

therefore, there was no way so many people could be actual witches. Though the Connecticut executions started up again in 1661 while Winthrop was in England, he fought for an end to the mass hysteria upon his return. Gradually, the magistrates were convinced to act more reasonably and look objectively at the evidence. Conviction could no longer rely on only one witness's testimony of a supernatural event; two people had to witness it at the same time. Since this was rarely the case, most testimonies were thrown out. New England entered a quiet period from 1663 to 1688 in which there were no executions and few accusations.

THE WATER TEST

Early Americans devised "tests" to determine whether an accused person was a witch. One was the water test, in which the accused's hands and feet were bound and her body dropped into deep water. If innocent and pure, God's water would accept her, and she would sink.

The problem? Few early Americans could swim. The accused would drown and onlookers were helpless to save her. If, however, she was a witch, the water would reject her and she would float. Though the accused survived the water test, they'd be hanged for the crime of witchcraft.

ATTEMPT TO DROWN A SUPPOSED WITCH

Early witch trials sometimes subjected accused witches to a water test, which people believed were proof of God's judgment as to whether the accused was pure or a witch.

THE FINAL TRIAL

In 1706, the last witch trial happened in America. In Virginia, a forty-six-year-old woman named Grace Sherwood, a midwife, widow, healer, and mother, was charged with witchcraft. Witnesses accused her of cursing crops, causing the death of livestock, harming her patients, and other acts. To prove her innocence or guilt, she was "ducked" in the Lynnhaven River, which was considered "consecrated" water (water blessed by God). Bound and weighted by a Bible, Sherwood was thrown from a boat into the water at an area now known as Witchduck Point. She managed to undo her bindings and float to the surface, whereupon she was immediately charged as a witch and jailed for seven years. After her release, Sherwood returned home and lived with her family until she died at age eighty. However, her name was not cleared until July 10, 2006, in a formal document signed by Virginia governor Tim Kaine.

THE BELL WITCH

Many years after Grace Sherwood was accused and jailed for her alleged witchcraft, a haunting believed to be witnessed and documented by hundreds of people, among them future president Andrew Jackson, represents one of the most famous instances of paranormal events in history. The alleged events took place between 1817 and 1821 and involved a family's belief that a witch plagued their lives.

The Bell family owned a farm near the Bell Witch Cave near Adams, Tennessee, and alleged a witch tormented them for years

The great-great-great-great-grandson of John Bell, Carney Bell, stands by a historical marker detailing the incredible story of the infamous Bell Witch legend, which involved his nineteenth-century ancestors in Tennessee.

and finally retreated to the cave for safety. The paranormal activities happened on the family's farm, though; the cave is not directly involved with the haunting.

DISTURBING ACTIVITIES

In 1804, the Bell family moved to a 320-acre farm in Tennessee along the Red River. They belonged to the local church and were active within the community. Their lives were uneventful until 1817, when strange things began to happen. One day, John Bell found a beast on his farm that seemed unnatural. He described it as having the body of a dog and the head of a rabbit. Confused, he shot the animal and it vanished. He forgot about the incident until his children complained of hearing rats gnawing on their bed and making noises around the house. Bell could not find a source of the noises. During several frightening encounters with the unseen terror, his daughter, Betsy, allegedly experienced hair pulling and assaults. She developed marks on her body as though she'd been whipped. Bedclothes were tossed around and pulled off the children during the night. Whispering voices added to the family's growing hysteria.

Though unnerved, the Bells hid these strange occurrences from others for a year. Then some neighbors stayed at the Bells' house and experienced the terrifying events themselves. They told John Bell to share his secret and allow people to investigate. This only seemed to strengthen the spirit. In some records, the spirit spoke and communicated with people. Its name was Kate, and Kate had only one mission: to kill John Bell and stop the marriage between his daughter and a local boy.

Bell died in 1820 of an apparent poisoning, and Betsy ended the engagement. The circumstances surrounding Bell's death were very mysterious.

THE BELL WITCH'S TRUE IDENTITY

Who was the Bell Witch? Speculation fell on Kate Batts, a neighbor of the Bells', who thought Bell had cheated her in a purchase of land and, upon suing him, vowed to haunt him and his descendants.

Though the Bell house has been torn down, many believe the spirit still haunts the land. The mystery of the Bell Witch has never been solved.

5

WITCHES: A CULTURAL PHENOMENON

Witches are an integral part of the United States' cultural heritage. This is due in part to the history of persecution of witches but also because of their prominence in popular culture. Witches can be found in very early literature. In the ancient Greek poem the *Odyssey*, an enchantress named Circe turns Odysseus's sailors into animals. From ancient literature to modern movies and television shows, the subject of witchcraft has been thoroughly explored.

THE WRITTEN WORD

From Nathaniel Hawthorne's *The House of Seven Gables* (1851) to the modern novels *Beautiful Creatures* (2010) and *The Graces*

(2016), authors have taken on witches with purpose and imagination. For those who are interested, there are many books to explore.

NARNIA

C. S. Lewis's *Chronicles of Narnia* series has been read and interpreted in dozens of ways since its publication in the 1950s. Its simple themes of good, evil, honor, and betrayal ring true across generations. In the magical land of Narnia, the brave and good lion named Aslan battles the evil White Witch—a classic literary approach to the supposed dark forces of witchcraft.

WITCHES AS ALLIES

Author Philip Pullman chose to portray witches as friends and allies to humans. In fact, his view of good and evil in his series, *His Dark Materials*, are quite different from those of other contemporary fantasy series. In his books, people's souls exist outside their bodies in the form of animals called dæmons. The world is

A COMMENTARY ON REAL LIFE

Witches have played a part in literature for centuries and served as plot devices for authors exploring life, history, and the supernatural. Shakespeare wrote about the king of Scotland and the English witch hysteria to portray the three Weird Sisters in *Macbeth*. Arthur Miller wrote *The Crucible* (1953) to comment on the McCarthy trials of the 1950s, in which many Americans were accused of Communism. The McCarthy trials have been called a "witch hunt," and Miller used his book to draw parallels to colonial Massachusetts. In 1996, *The Crucible* was adapted into a major feature film.

run by an authoritative religious group known as the Magisterium. A witch queen named Serafina Pekkala warns of a place called Bolvanger, where children are being cut away from their dæmons so they will never experience sin. Serafina offers to help Lyra, the main character, in her quest to save the other children.

THE *HARRY POTTER* SERIES

The *Harry Potter* books perhaps best illustrate and redefine classic stereotypes of witches and witchcraft. Witches exist in Harry's world, but in secret, with an entire government office devoted to

Daniel Radcliffe played Harry Potter in 2001's *Harry Potter and the Sorcerer's Stone*, as well as its sequels. Modern-day witchcraft stories often portray witches and wizards as both good and evil beings in varying degrees of supernatural circumstances.

the practice of witchcraft. At a magical school, Hogwarts, young wizards and witches learn how to use their magical powers and the basics of herbology, potions, and divination—subjects that hearken back to stereotypical practices of witches, which prove useful in combating evil. Harry's world is portrayed as normal and parallel to the real world, with a few differences.

In preparation for Hogwarts, Harry obtains stereotypical witch-craft items: a cauldron, a pointed hat, a familiar (an owl), and a wand. Harry's nemesis, a dark lord named Voldemort, leads a pack of evil wizards who are marked by a symbol on their wrists, similar to how things like birthmarks supposedly indicated someone was a witch in the Middle Ages and in early America. Some characters are shape-shifters, another stereotypical power of witches. Good and evil are given equal play in the series, and both appeal to Harry at different times in his life at Hogwarts.

WICKED

There is another side to the story of the Wicked Witch of the West villainized in the 1939 movie *The Wizard of Oz*, thanks to a book called *Wicked: The Life and Times of the Wicked Witch of the West* (1995) by Gregory Maguire. (It was made into a wildly pop-ular Broadway musical called *Wicked*.) Elphaba is a young witch with green skin who is friends with a beautiful young witch named Glinda. Themes of alienation, bullying, and intolerance run through the story and echo the persecutions suffered by accused witches throughout history.

ON TV

Television has brought a new visual element to the iconic witch. In witch-centered television, magic is used for everything from good, everyday activities to supernatural and frightening purposes.

FRIENDLY TELEVISION PORTRAYALS

In series such as *Bewitched, Sabrina: The Teenage Witch,* and *The Chilling Adventures of Sabrina,* attractive women are portrayed as witches rather than the old hags from folklore and fairy tales. In the Syfy series *Merlin,* the legendary King Arthur and his adviser, a wizard named Merlin, fight for their places in the world. Magic

Kiernan Shipka plays the half-human, half-witch title character in Netflix's *The Chilling Tales of Sabrina.* Far from the wart-ridden old hags long used to depict witches, Sabrina is a young woman trying to balance her supernatural powers with a regular teeenager's life.

is kept hidden and secret, but it is also intrinsic and essential to Arthur's ascension to the throne of Camelot. As with the *Harry Potter* series, *Merlin*'s focus is more on wizards than witches.

The 2013 Disney Channel movie *Descendants* explores the lives of the children of various villainous Disney witches, such as Maleficent from *Sleeping Beauty*.

HISTORICAL FICTION TO FANTASY

Witches feature in various frightening and historically inspired contexts in other television shows, many of which are based on books. In Netflix's *The Last Kingdom,* based on Bernard Cornwell's historical fiction series *The Saxon Tales,* witches among the Vikings invading Britain are used in an attempt to secure Viking successes over the native Saxons and Britons. In the Starz series *Outlander,* based on Diana Gabaldon's historical time travel series of the same name, the main character is transported to eighteenth-century Scotland, where accused witches were arrested and executed. In HBO's *Game of Thrones,* based on George R. R. Martin's fantasy series *A Song of Ice and Fire,* historical themes of healers being accused of witchcraft and sorcery are key plot elements.

FILMS

Movies have great influence over how the audience views magic and witchcraft. Feature-length re-imaginings of books and original screenplays transport viewers to all kinds of enchanted locations: Mordor and the Shire in *The Lord of the Rings*, the island of Tortuga

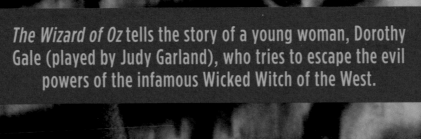

The Wizard of Oz tells the story of a young woman, Dorothy Gale (played by Judy Garland), who tries to escape the evil powers of the infamous Wicked Witch of the West.

in *Pirates of the Caribbean*, and France in Disney's *Beauty and the Beast*. Classic fairy tales involving witches have been adapted in modern movies, such as 2014's *Maleficent* and *Into The Woods*, which features adaptations of various folklore as well as the witch-themed classics, *Sleeping Beauty* and *Snow White*.

THE WIZARD OF OZ

The Emerald City is the destination in this classic movie. A stunning retelling of the favorite book *The Wonderful Wizard of Oz* (1900) by L. Frank Baum, this film performs an interesting trick of foreshadowing by casting Margaret Hamilton as both Almira Gulch, the nasty neighbor in Kansas who is bitten by Toto and tries to take him away, and the Wicked Witch of the West in Oz. The familiar touchstones of an evil witch—a pointy hat, green skin, mean disposition, and flying broomstick (that is mirrored in the bicycle Gulch rides during the tornado)—are featured.

THE LITTLE MERMAID

In Disney's retelling of the Hans Christian Andersen fairy tale, a young mermaid with a beautiful singing voice named Ariel longs to be human to be with the prince she rescued in the ocean. She turns to an old, plump sea witch named Ursula, who longs to be young, pretty, and have a beautiful singing voice again. Ursula exacts a heavy price from Ariel in exchange for giving the young mermaid the ability to walk on land and meet her prince. Ursula is portrayed as evil, selfish, vindictive, and jealous—a stereotypical witch.

BIBLIOGRAPHY

Becker, Marshall J. "An American Witch Bottle." Archaeological Institute of America. Retrieved February 15, 2019. http://www.archaeology.org/online/features/halloween/witch_bottle.html.

Greek Mythology. "Circe." Retrieved February 15, 2019. https://www.greekmythology.com/Other_Gods/Circe/circe.html.

Hamilton, John. *Witches*. Edina, MN: ABDO Publishing Company, 2007.

Illes, Judika. *The Weiser Field Guide to Witches: From Hexes to Hermione Granger, from Salem to the Land of Oz.* San Francisco, CA: Red Wheel/Weiser, 2010.

Lynette, Rachel. *Witches*. Farmington Hills, MI: Thomson Gale, 2007.

Malam, John. *Monster Mania: Witches*. Irvine, CA: QEB Publishing, 2010.

McDougald-Williams, Erin. "America's Most Haunted Location: Bell Witch Cave." Suite101.com. August 31, 2010. http://www.suite101.com/content/americas-most-haunted-location-bell-witch-cave-a280783.

Meltzer, Milton. *Witches and Witch-hunts: A History of Persecution.* New York, NY: The Blue Sky Press, 1999.

Murphy-Hiscock, Arin. *The Way of the Hedge Witch: Rituals and Spells for Hearth and Home.* Avon, MA: Adams Media, 2009.

Nardo, Don. *The Salem Witch Trials*. Farmington Hills, MI: Lucent Books, 2007.

Stark, Bruce P. "Witchcraft in Connecticut." Connecticut's Heritage Gateway. Retrieved February 11, 2011. http://www.ctheritage .org/encyclopedia/ctto1763/witchcraft.htm.

Virginia Historical Society. "The 'Witch of Pungo': 300 Years After Her Conviction, Governor Restores Grace Sherwood's Good Name." Retrieved February 11, 2011. http://www.vahistorical .org/news/gracesherwood.htm.

"Witches and Wizards." Myths Encyclopedia: Myths and Legends of the World. Retrieved February 11, 2011. http://www .mythencyclopedia.com/Wa-Z/Witches-and-Wizards.html.

Woodward, Walter P. "New England's Other Witch-hunt: The Hartford Witch-hunt of the 1660s and Changing Patterns in Witchcraft Prosecution." Organization of American Historians Magazine of History. Retrieved February 11, 2011. http://maghis .oxfordjournals.org/content/17/4/16.ful.

GLOSSARY

alchemy A medieval chemical science that aims to transform base metals into gold.

astrology The study of stars in terms of how they influence human life and behavior.

deity In a polytheistic religion, a god or goddess; in monotheism, a supreme being.

familiar An animal, often a cat, believed to assist witches in their magic.

hysteria A form of mental illness that causes wild behavior and physical problems and sometimes spreads to others, known as mass hysteria.

pagan A follower of a religion that believes in many gods.

paranormal Events or phenomena that can't be explained by normal, accepted science.

Puritan A member of a sixteenth- and seventeenth-century Protestant group in England and New England that opposed ceremonial worship and practiced a strict moral code.

sabbath A superstitious midnight meeting of witches with the Devil.

sermon A religious speech, usually discussing a biblical message or belief and delivered by a clergy member.

shape-shifting The ability of one being to assume the shape and appearance of another through magic or supernatural means.

specter A ghost or disembodied spirit.

spell A spoken enchantment.

superstition A belief or practice resulting from ignorance, fear of the unknown, or trust in magic or chance.

Wicca A pagan religion influenced by ancient, pre-Christian beliefs that affirms the existence of supernatural powers, multiple deities, and emphasizes ritual observance of seasonal and life cycles.

witch A person who practices magic.

witchcraft The use of sorcery or magic.

FURTHER READING

BOOKS

Horsley, Katherine. *Investigating Magic*. New York, NY: Rosen Publishing, 2017.

Light, Kate. *Questions and Answers About the Salem Witch Trials*. New York, NY: PowerKids Press, 2019.

Marsico, Katie. *Magic Monsters: From Witches to Goblins*. Minneapolis, MN: Lerner Publishing Group, 2017.

Peterson, Megan Cooley. *The Bell Witch: An American Ghost Story*. North Mankato, MN: Capstone Press, 2019.

WEBSITES

Academic Kids: Witch-hunt

academickids.com/encyclopedia/index.php/Witch-hunt

Read more about the history of witch hunts around the world.

Kiddle: Wicca Facts for Kids

kids.kiddle.co/Wicca

Learn more about Wicca, the modern religion dedicated to ancient practices related to magic.

National Geographic Kids: The Salem Witch Trials

kids.nationalgeographic.com/explore/history/salem-witch-trials

Dive deeper into the Salem witch trials and see photos and illustrations.

INDEX